SHERLOCK HOLMES

10 MINUTE PLAYS

John DeGaetano

Based on the original books by Sir Arthur Conan Doyle

Elizabeth at the age of 8

SHERLOCK HOLMES

10-MINUTE PLAYS

ALL Stories by John DeGaetano,
Based on the original books by Sir Arthur Conan Doyle
© July 2012

About the Author

John DeGaetano, Theater Stage Director in the San Francisco Bay Area re-creates his twist on three new Sherlock Holmes adventures in the *10 Minute Plays*. Based in part from the career writings of Holmes' long time friend Dr. Watson. The playwright, whose witty, well-crafted scripts are homage to Conan Doyle and the great pleasure in seeing his iconic characters, brought to life. Each play is just 10 minutes in length, four to six characters, simple unit set requirements and suitable for all audiences.

Sherlock Holmes and The Prisoner's Mystery – *It's up to Holmes and Dr. Watson to solve an unusual case of a man accused of a crime he did not commit and attempts to clear his name.*

Sherlock Holmes and A Case of Revenge – *Holmes himself is puzzled why a woman seeks revenge for a famous mans death... We can't tell you any more than that in this emotional 10-Minute thriller.*

Sherlock Holmes and the Darkness Upon Us – *A man searching for the organizer of a much larger crime turns up dead at the Voodoo Sea Hag Pub as Holmes and Dr. Watson are called in to uncover the mystery.*

A delightful evening of entertainment and mystery lie ahead as you're taken back to Victorian England and the untidy flat at 221-B Baker Street. Many of you have enjoyed his full-length play *Sherlock Holmes and the Princess Jewel,* and now you can experience here the entirely new short play scripts series *Mr. DeGaetano* has crafted. There's plenty of intrigue and adventure, as the stories move quickly which are guaranteed to please everyone who joins in.

For more information on these and other items please visit our website: johndegaetanoproductions.com

SHERLOCK HOLMES and THE PRISONER'S MYSTERY

Story by John DeGaetano,
Based on the original books by Sir Arthur Conan Doyle
© June 2012 v:1.2

Type: A Mystery Play
Stage Time Length: 10 Minutes

Cast: 4 men, 2 women:
Set: Flexible Room and Office Setting
(221-B Baker Street, London England)

Cast of Characters:
SHERLOCK HOLMES
DOCTOR WATSON
MRS. HUDSON
MRS. SARAH WALKER
CHIEF INSPECTOR LESTRADE
SERGEANT COLLINS

For Stage Production use or more Information
Contact Email: degaetanojohn@yahoo.com
Website: johndegaetanoproductions.com
Phone: 707-338-2886

THE SCENE: (Begins on a summer afternoon in Baker Street at the conclusion of one of Mrs. Hudson's lunches. Holmes is napping after the meal and Watson is comfortable in a chair with a newspaper up to his face reading the content)

SOUND: (The sound of Holmes snoring, pause, then a loud sneeze by Watson)

HOLMES: (Awakes, obviously startled by the sound in his chair) A bit of a cold Watson?

WATSON: On the contrary my good man, so sorry to have startled you.

HOLMES: (Clears his throat as he starts to move about in his chair) More like an allergic reaction…

WATSON: Wrong again old chap… just a summer sneeze.

HOLMES: You did come in from the garden, did you not?

WATSON: Yes…

HOLMES: And, the gentle breeze in a westerly direction, if I'm not mistaken…

WATSON: Ah, well… um, why yes. Oh rubbish, (annoyed) what does that have to do with it?

HOLMES: Then, I would be correct in recognizing that within your jacket lapel lodges pollen (moves closer to look at his jacket) from the cherry blossom flower that headed to your fashionable attire from a westerly direction as you watered the rest.

WATSON: (Looks at his sleeve) Yes, yes… Holmes very observant… (Amused)

HOLMES: Thus allergies have bitten you my good man.

WATSON: Why yes... I do believe so.

(There is a knock at the door and Mrs. Hudson enters)

HOLMES: Yes, do come in Mrs. Hudson.

MRS. HUDSON: Mr. Holmes there is a woman somewhat ruffled in appearance asking to see you gentlemen?

WATSON: Oh really... now who might that be?

HOLMES: Ruffled appearance my good man Watson, leads me to believe she is in need of some help, possibly a missing persons... no, rather someone that has been missed for a long time... on second thought someone who is dead.

MRS. HUDSON: Mr. Holmes I see you liked my meat pie. Well doctor, you hardly touched yours!

HOLMES: Understandably the recipe has been tested enough to allow one to over eat with enjoyment and then fall fast asleep.

WATSON: Which he did...

HOLMES: Which I did, indeed...

WATSON: Lost my appetite, my reason is blasted allergies, you know?

MRS. HUDSON: Oh really doctor I didn't know you suffered.

WATSON: Oh but I do Mrs. Hudson... ah, Cherry blossoms to be exact. Holmes I'm intrigued to see if you are the least bit correct having never seen this woman.

HOLMES: She'll be wearing a shawl to protect her from a slight wind...

WATSON: Westerly I gather…

HOLMES: Correct, and I suspect from the Soho district; poor… made it here on foot, kind disposition, a gentle beauty. Please do send her in Mrs. Hudson.

MRS. HUDSON: Very well Mr. Holmes.

(Emerges in the doorway is Mrs. Walker, looking exactly as Holmes described)

MRS. WALKER: Good afternoon Mr. Holmes… Dr. Watson (They both stand)

WATSON: Do come in Miss… ah… Miss, ah…

MRS. WALKER: Walker… Mrs. Sarah Walker.

WATSON: Please sit down Mrs. Walker, make yourself comfortable… what can we do for you my dear lady?

MRS. WALKER: So kind of you gentlemen to see me without notice… I walked here thinking of this crazy notion that you are the only ones that can help me in this situation.

HOLMES: How so Mrs. Walker?

MRS. WALKER: You see, my husband Nigel was convicted of a crime he did not commit.

WATSON; I'm sure he had proper representation Mrs. Walker?

MRS. WALKER: Oh yes he did… however counsel could not prove he did not commit the murder.

WATSON: Murder? Good heavens.

8

MRS. WALKER: That was over fifteen years ago… Mr. Holmes, are you familiar with the Colonel De Brie case?

HOLMES: Yes… yes, Mrs. Walker. Colonel De Brie was murdered in 1882; he was the great grandson of French King Louis-Philippe, the founder of the French Foreign Legion.

MRS. WALKER: That is correct, the Colonel became quite wealthy in his later years as a businessman in the gems trade, lived a lavish life however I'm told his early years were as unconventional as it gets.

HOLMES: I see… go on.

MRS. WALKER: In any case, the estate is not far from here, just a short walk. His mansion on the night I speak of was ransacked and the Colonel was subsequently murdered.

HOLMES: Correct, I remember, your husband was found guilty of the robbery and therefore was linked to the murder, a wealth of jewels were never recovered.

MRS. WALKER: Quite right… however, my husband did not murder Colonel De Brie and spent fourteen years in jail attempting to clear his name. Until his death that is… I have been a widow for exactly one year. In fact it wasn't until yesterday that I received this note in post from a Rachel Mills.

WATSON: Rachel Mills? Was that not the Colonel's mistress, ah, friend… something or other, what have you? She moved away after the murder if I am not mistaken.

HOLMES: Ah yes… they never married thus not an heir to his fortune. Mrs. Walker, would you be so kind as to read its contents.

MRS. WALKER: Yes… it reads. "Dear Mrs. Walker… I lie here on my deathbed, as I realize I am not a good woman nor will my health ever improve. I have done a terrible thing. It was my own jealously and greed that provoked me in killing Colonel Jean Claude De Brie the night of the robbery so many years ago. I remain now gasping for air in confessing the truth, in hopes that your husband can be freed. Forgive me… Signed… Rachel Mills."

WATSON: Interesting… Mrs. Walker, have you contacted the authorities upon receiving this note?

MRS. WALKER: Why no Mr. Holmes… I… (Interrupted)

HOLMES: Excuse me…. Mrs. Hudson… (Yells for Mrs. Hudson as he turns back to Mrs. Walker) we must get some clarification on the case

MRS. HUDSON: (Opens the door) Yes Mr. Holmes.

HOLMES: Will you kindly summon Chief Inspector Lestrade immediately?

MRS. HUDSON: Well, well fancy that Mr. Holmes… he is just outside across the street as we speak.

HOLMES: My dear Mrs. Walker I suspect you have been followed here, if the jewels have never been recovered then Scotland Yard believes you may know of their location.

MRS. WALKER: I have no idea of their whereabouts… I do know Mr. Holmes that my husband after losing his job as a skilled craftsman did what he could to feed our family.

WATSON: An incredibly tough time for all…

MRS. WALKER: He was kind and gentle man; work got harder and harder to find. I know he did not always make the right choices… there was always that desperation look in his eyes.

WATSON: Rightly so… losing ones job amounts to desperation.

HOLMES: If I'm correct in De Brie's history, he left his schooling, pushed by his family and inevitably joined the French Foreign Legion. He spent his years fighting and was almost continually in action against someone or another of the revolting native tribes in Morocco, and other areas where the Legion was then heavily engaged.

WATSON: Yes, right around the time I was commissioned in the Army's Medical Department he was stationed somewhere in the Middle Atlas Mountains... and French outposts.

HOLMES: Shot in the left leg he recovered quickly however resigned his commission and over the next three decades developed and rose to become one of the leading players in the growing Far East gem trade business that made him a very wealthy man.

(Inspector Lestrade enters, listens in and picks up the conversation)

LESTRADE: So a few years later he set his sights on London where he purchased a mansion estate coincidentally not far from your Baker Street residence here, moved his fortune in jewels to England. Never married though as the story goes. Why good afternoon gentlemen... I hear you have requested to see me?

HOLMES: Yes, yes... Inspector Lestrade, how good to see you please do come in. May I introduce Mrs. Walker?

LESTRADE: Why yes... Mrs. Walker, the wife of Nigel Walker. This must be why we are talking about Colonel De Brie.

HOLMES: Inspector you remember the sequence of events?

LESTRADE: I certainly do, there was no real solid evidence that your husband committed the crime. My conclusion was he had motive as the courts ruled... to commit robbery and was caught in the act.

HOLMES: Until now Inspector, Mrs. Walkers holds a note from the Colonel's mistress; I who assume has since died. Although it won't be difficult to verify the writing (Mrs. Walker hands Lestrade the note)

LESTRADE: Mmmm... I see, (As he reads) but why though, after all these years the woman comes forward?

MRS. WALKER: Inspector my husband never spoke of the woman nor did he ever admit even to me of the murder. He did say he wanted to provide for his family any way he could... and there was always a market to a network of crime from what he could gather.

WATSON: Yes, we know where that leads one, but how utterly questionable this Rachel Mills' intentions in the matter.

HOLMES: Yes very curious.

LESTRADE: How so Doctor?

WATSON: Well, there are several questions to ask here. To start, why after all this time did the mistress come forward? Why did your husband not implicate her in the crime if he did not commit it?

HOLMES: Yes... reasonable questions indeed Watson. Ah, Mrs. Walker did your husband leave any belongings upon his death... anything to speak of?

MRS. WALKER: Yes Mr. Holmes... a pencil, a small notepad and an old pocket watch. As I said I've been a widow for one year and just now his belongings were returned to me.

LESTRADE: Normal procedure Madame, I recall this formality is in place in case anyone comes forward to state claim on the items. In this case your husband had very few keepsakes.

HOLMES: Do you have these articles with you and may I examine them Mrs. Walker?

MRS. WALKER: But of course Mr. Holmes (The lady reaches into her bag and presents an envelope containing the items, removes them and hands them to Holmes). A pencil, a small notepad and an old pocket watch.

WATSON: And a letter from Rachel Mills… that is what we have to go on…

HOLMES: Correct Watson… very curious, the pencil is short obviously for writing yet the note pad is blank.

MRS. WALKER: Except Mr. Holmes for the very last page that reads "My love to our family."

HOLMES: Yes… (Turns to that page and pauses heavy in thought as he hands it to Watson, then Watson to Lestrade). And the watch Mrs. Walker…

MRS. WALKER: Of no real value… he constantly carried it with him… for years. (She hands it to Holmes)

HOLMES: I see… yes, quite tattered (examines the item and opens the lid to read the inscription) "My dearest, see you at eight," any significance Mrs. Walker to this statement?

MRS. WALKER: Just to me… that was our statement to one another when we first met… it was at eight in the evening. Before our marriage, during those evenings, that was our time to meet. Sometimes Nigel would attempt to impress me with a gift, a thought or something amusing to show his deep affection for me.

HOLMES: And the scribed lines on the back of the watch? (Hands the watch to Watson)

MRS. WALKER: Honestly Mr. Holmes, I never examined his watch. It was always his, in his pocket that is… I don't recall any significance.

WATSON: Fascinating… (Also examines the item)

HOLMES: Ah Inspector... Can you tell me about the Colonel's Manson?

LESTRADE: Well, there is nothing to tell, a large structure... the property sits...

HOLMES: Sits on an unusual lot, am I correct?

LESTRADE: Well, ah... yes, that is correct.

HOLMES: With six corners... Watson do we have a record of maps in that pile of reference?

WATSON: I do believe so. (Stands up to look for the book)

LESTRADE: Let me see... you may be correct Holmes. If I remember correctly the property was deeded to the Colonel and some of the adjoining parcels as well. I'm told he cherished his privacy.

(Watson returns holding a large book of maps, sets it on the table, they all crowd around to look at it, Mrs. Walker remains seated)

HOLMES: (Holmes turns the pages with vigor, then sets his eyes in one area of the large page) Curious Watson...

WATSON: What do you mean old man?

HOLMES: You see these scribed lines on the back of the watch?

WATSON: Yes...

HOLMES: They closely resemble the boundary lines on the Colonel's property (points) here, here, here and so on...

WATSON: Could it be? I... I do believe you may be... (Interrupted)

HOLMES: Inspector I gather your Sergeant is just outside our door?

LESTRADE: That is correct Holmes.

HOLMES: Then would you be so kind as to ask him to assist us?

LESTRADE: But of course... (Exits to retrieve the Sergeant)

HOLMES: Splendid... Mrs. Walker, you just received these items from the prison so they were not tampered with in any way?

MRS. WALKER: Why no, Mr. Holmes... they are exactly how I received them. Why do you ask?

HOLMES: Very well then. My dear lady, I believe that the hands of the watch were put in this position intentionally. They point exactly to the number ten for the hour hand and to the number two for the minute hand.

MRS. WALKER: Yes... is that of any significance?

WATSON: Holmes, in some cultures the hands of a clock express an emotion. In this case the positioning could mean happiness, or a smile or good fortune.

HOLMES: Precisely Watson!!! There is a one in seven hundred and twenty chance the hands would be in this precise position. Now then, Watson if you will assist me.

WATSON: (Watson now studies the map) All right... if we assume this point to be north as it corresponds to the inscription, then based on the map coordinates: the parcel is three hundred and twenty paces from the ten-hand position to the two-hand position... right... there. (Points)

MRS. WALKER: Amazing gentlemen...

WATSON: Now what Holmes?

HOLMES: My dear Watson fine work... now, the inscription on the lid "My dearest, see you at eight" if we follow a similar format from the eight-hand to the twelve... what do we come up with?

(Lestrade now enters with Sergeant Collins and they join everyone at the table)

WATSON: (Vigorously counting) Three... that would be four hundred and forty paces according to my calculations.

HOLMES: Gentlemen and Lady... "X" marks the spot... approximately ninety paces from the west and one hundred and ten paces from the north.

LESTRADE: Amazing Holmes... Sergeant, if you please?

SERGEANT COLLINS: Yes, right away sir, I will bring the men to these coordinates: Ninety paces from the west due east and one hundred and ten paces from the north due south. (Exits)

WATSON: Thank you Sergeant.

HOLMES: I think you may find what has been missing for over fifteen years Inspector. Was this an amusement so to speak from your husband Mrs. Walker?

MRS. WALKER: The jewels were never recovered... so there is a good chance of it.

HOLMES: Here is the speculation however... if the jewels are in fact at this location, your husband may have been commissioned to perform the theft.

MRS. WALKER: I understand this may have been the case.

WATSON: If this is the case Rachel Mills performed the murder in the cover of the robbery.

LESTRADE: I see... then your husband not knowing he was part of a bigger crime was accused of the murder and from that he refused to share the fortune

WATSON: Leaving the double-crosser, in this case Colonel De Brie's mistress in poverty and homeless.

HOLMES: Correct gentlemen!

MRS. WALKER: This revelation is reassuring... my husband's name could be cleared.

HOLMES: Mrs. Walker, your husband's name WILL be cleared, if nothing else by the written letter.

LESTRADE: That is correct Mrs. Walker... I will personally verify its authenticity and clearance of your husband's name.

MRS. WALKER: I really don't know what to say but to thank you gentlemen.

WATSON: My dear lady, I see you have suffered all these years with the pain that your husband could have committed this murder... now your thoughts are freed. (Sergeant Collins reenters, out of breath)

SERGEANT COLLINS: Sir we have found something... Mr. Holmes, I think you have solved a fifteen-year mystery.

WATSON: Fascinating!

LESTRADE: Good work Sergeant... I will accompany you to verify the location and contents. Mrs. Walker, gentlemen, I think my work is done here... good evening.

HOLMES: You are correct Inspector Lestrade and thank you for your help. (The Inspector and the Sergeant exit)

MRS. WALKER: What an amazing turn of events Mr. Holmes, Doctor Watson...

HOLMES: Oh by the way Mrs. Walker, you may want to take this with you. (Holmes hands her a small pouch) You see your husband engraved the case with the concaved end of the pencil and a diamond.

MRS. WALKER: A diamond... What are you talking about?

HOLMES: You have five children isn't that correct?

MRS. WALKER: Why yes, but I never spoke of them... so how did you know?

HOLMES: I think you'll find in the pouch there are six diamonds, one very large one and five of equal size. You see your husband as you said was indeed a craftsman. The watch has a secret compartment that opens when you apply pressure to the back of the case in the vicinity of each of the numbers ten, twelve, two and eight.

MRS. WALKER: You cannot be serious...

HOLMES: Oh but I am, they are of good size... and they are yours Mrs. Walker. I suspect one to two carats each. They should fetch a good amount for you and your family...

WATSON: Maybe your husband meant to say... "See you at eight... carats" (They all laugh)

The End

SHERLOCK HOLMES and A CASE OF REVENGE

Story by John DeGaetano,
Based on the original books by Sir Arthur Conan Doyle
© June 2012 v:1.2

Type: A Mystery Play
Stage Time Length: 10 Minutes

Cast: 2 men, 2 women:
Set: Flexible Room and Office Setting
(221-B Baker Street, London England)

Cast of Characters:
SHERLOCK HOLMES
DOCTOR WATSON
MRS. HUDSON
ELIZABETH CRAWFORD

For Stage Production use or more Information
Contact Email: degaetanojohn@yahoo.com
Website: johndegaetanoproductions.com
Phone: 707-338-2886

THE SCENE: (Begins on a cool afternoon in Baker Street at the conclusion of a game of chess. Holmes picks up the violin and plays softy while Watson is comfortable in a chair with a newspaper and heavy in thought)

SOUND: (The sound of Holmes playing the violin, pause, then a loud sound of a book falling off a shelf)

HOLMES: (Distracted, moves to the bookshelf) The wind moves in mysterious ways, wouldn't you say Watson?

WATSON: Interesting my good man, how a somewhat heavy item as that to essentially take flight and move it's location.

HOLMES: (Set his violin down and moves to a chair) In retrospect the wind has inspired mythology, influenced the events of history, expanded the range of transport and warfare, and moves the smallest of particles...

WATSON: Yes, to include a book's sailing voyage off the shelf my good man. (Chuckles as Mrs. Hudson enters) Some things still remain unexplained...

MRS. HUDSON:
Only for now gentlemen... I can explain there is a chill in the air and the only remedy is a warm liquid. Are we all in agreement?

WATSON: Yes indeed, my dear Mrs. Hudson has anyone ever told you that you're very convincing?

MRS. HUDSON: Yes... my first suitor when I convinced him to kiss me under the oaks on a lovely summer eve.

HOLMES: And madam to his advantage he will always remember your attention to detail... possibly in a short story?

MRS. HUDSON: Why Mr. Holmes I do not know why I am here, when I could be in the countryside writing love stories.

BLACKWELL'S

Despatch Note

Thank you for visiting and ordering from www.blackwell.co.uk.

K Walker
33 Station Road
SOUTH QUEENSFERRY
West Lothian
EH30 9HZ
United Kingdom

Order number: 002241006
Despatch date: 05 Jan 2017
Delivery method: Priority
Total books: 1
Total price: 10.58

Qty	ISBN	Title	Price	Disc	Net	VAT	Subtotal
1	9781477616123	Sherlock Holmes 10 Minute Plays	7.08	0.00	7.08	0.00	10.58

Personal Message

Returns: If you need to return your book, simply log onto your account on the site and then click onto your order. Fill in the returns form and use the sticker below when you are posting back the book. If you have any problems please email our Customer Services team at **blackwell.online@blackwell.co.uk**

BWSS Returns: 002241006

Blackwell Online
50 Broad Street
Oxford
OX1 3BQ
U.K.

PLEASE HANDLE WITH CARE

WATSON: One can dream… can't they?

MRS. HUDSON: Correct… and gentlemen in the meantime I will dream up dinner for the evening downstairs in anticipation to that kind of eventual adventure (Suddenly, there is a knock at the door downstairs) All right! (At the doorway, yelling down the landing) I'm coming…

HOLMES: Very well Mrs. Hudson. (Mrs. Hudson reappears at the door and enters)

HOLMES: Yes has someone called, Mrs. Hudson?

MRS. HUDSON: Yes, Mr. Holmes there is a woman at the door that has requested to see you.

WATSON: Is that so… well, seeing that the afternoon has been somewhat uneventful, I for one can use some stimulating conversation… would you agree Holmes?

HOLMES: Mrs. Hudson… what is she wearing?

MRS. HUDSON: Now Mr. Holmes, how do you expect me to remember that?

WATSON: Oh rubbish Holmes… you will find out soon enough!

HOLMES: Mrs. Hudson… have I taught you nothing in screening your visitors? (Smiles) Very well, please do send her in.

WATSON: Good… I'm glad we all agree with that…

MRS. HUDSON: Very well Mr. Holmes. (In an undertone) My visitors, ha!

(Emerges in the doorway is Miss Elizabeth Crawford, pretty, well spoken, neatly dressed middle aged woman. Mrs. Hudson eventually follows her in with tea service)

ELIZABETH: Good afternoon Mr. Holmes... Dr. Watson (They both stand)

WATSON: Do come in Miss... ah... Miss, ah

ELIZABETH: My name is Crawford... Elizabeth Crawford, thank you Mrs. Hudson. Such a chilling day, and tea certainly warms the nerves.

MRS. HUDSON: You are very welcomed young lady. (Smiles)

WATSON: Please be seated Miss Crawford (Watson takes the tea service from Mrs. Hudson and begins to serve everyone) Yes... and what can we do for you dear lady?

ELIZABETH: Thank you Mr. Holmes, Dr. Watson... (Watson hands the woman a cup of tea and then to Holmes) I have heard a great deal about you both.

HOLMES: Oh is that so?

ELIZABETH: Yes... my father and others have spoke very highly of you. I... ah, I would like to know if you could help me?

HOLMES: Possibly... please tell us what is on your mind?

ELIZABETH: Well, that fact of the matter is I would like to know if you would take on a missing person case?

HOLMES: A missing person you say?

ELIZABETH: Yes, you see... my father has since passed and I am trying to locate his old friend. I'm told my father carried a photo of me when I was eight years old.

HOLMES: I see... and who is your father, might I ask?

ELIZABETH: I do not know...

WATSON: Excuse me Miss Crawford... but you just said...

ELIZABETH: Please call me Elizabeth, I would like you to remember me by my first name and that is what I prefer to be called.

WATSON: Very well Elizabeth... You do not know your father?

ELIZABETH: That is correct... I never got to know him, however a man that attended school with him does... at least, that is what I am told.

WATSON: All right then... what is his name? (They all sip tea)

ELIZABETH: I do not know... nor do I know the school he later attended. I will be however meeting a gentleman very shortly who says he recalls my father when I was very young and at that time separated from him.

HOLMES: I suspect you do not know how or why you were separated as well?

ELIZABETH: That is correct; (Hesitates) my request here gentleman today is to merely inquire about your services to track down the information.

HOLMES: Very well Miss... a... Elizabeth, We are at your disposal and can attempt to help you when you can give us a bit more detail.

WATSON: Yes but the gentleman you're meeting... I would like to know... (Interrupted)

ELIZABETH: Splendid gentlemen... (Looks at her timepiece) oh my, my, look at the time. I really must be hurrying off. May I contact you shortly? I really must be running along... so sorry gentlemen. (The woman moves to the doorway and at the same time hands a card to Mrs. Hudson and quickly exits)

WATSON: Yes... all right (they all pause several beats, then look at each other). That was odd...

HOLMES: Odd indeed Watson...

MRS. HUDSON: What in Gods name was that about?

HOLMES: Quite an interesting study, that woman, Watson, I'm afraid we are in some sort of danger... She mentioned her father spoke of me, yet she does not know him.

WATSON: Danger you say... what sort of danger?

HOLMES: Her clothing style... different, not from this immediate area, nor was her way of speaking. She had a general air of being fairly well to do in an uncomfortable, yet set by the trappings of wealth sort of way.

WATSON: Yes, you observed a good deal about her, some not particularly visible to me. However I suspect from America... would you agree?

HOLMES: Yes... (Heavy in thought) the Midwest... she had working hands, farmer's hands but I suspect that was to throw us off. Her body movements, the flickering of her eyelid I believe says she was nervous and attempting to deceive us.

(Holmes sits silent for a few seconds with his fingertips still pressed against his lips, his legs squarely frontwards and his gaze directed upward to the ceiling)

WATSON: Odd... how absolutely... incredibly odd my good man. I suspect we will soon find out. Incidentally, Mrs. Hudson what did the woman hand you?

(Mrs. Hudson opens the envelope to reveal a card with a growing look of terror in her eyes)

HOLMES: Yes and in response to your statement Watson… no, not invisible to you but perhaps unnoticed in details at this point. The message should tie this whole affair together… Please read on Mrs. Hudson. (There is a pause)

WATSON: Mrs. Hudson, are you all right?

MRS. HUDSON: Ah, yes doctor… the note. The note reads:

"My dear Sherlock Holmes, I will be brief. I have waited for this day to meet you in more ways than one. Let me first tell you that you have merely ten maybe twelve minutes to live. You see you have all been poisoned."

WATSON: Good heavens! (Mrs. Hudson continues to read the note, terrified)

HOLMES: Continue Mrs. Hudson please… (Runs to look out the window)

MRS. HUDSON: "The toxin remains active for twenty-four hours thereby discouraging any immediate outside help. Now… I will say however that your Doctor Watson and your Mrs. Hudson have already been administered the antidote. They will live I suppose."

"You, on the other hand must, with your incredible brain of deduction attempt to find the antidote while simultaneously suffering in mind and body every second along the way. First losing the use of you legs, then continue on until you can barely blink an eye until you gasp for air."

HOLMES: Amazing turn of events wouldn't you say Watson? (They all look at each other in horror)

MRS. HUDSON: (Reads on) "You see Mr. Holmes, my father suffered. He could not endure to have you track him, day in and day out until then he confronted you directly. You remember? (Pause) You were the cause of his death... You now have approximately nine minutes to live. And so Mr. Holmes just as you poisoned my father's thoughts in life, I dedicated my efforts to return to you the favor."

HOLMES: Signed, Elizabeth... Moriarty not Crawford as previously said.

MRS. HUDSON: Yes, signed, Elizabeth Moriarty... My god! (Astonished)

WATSON: Ludicrous, the lady is Professor Moriarty's daughter?

HOLMES: Hardly a lady Watson, and I, at this point not one to question it. I do find this a bit more interesting than her little problem, which, by the way, was rather a trite one.

MRS. HUDSON: But Mr. Holmes there is very little time... what can we do?

HOLMES: Quick Watson... would you be so kind as to develop a coding system for blinking eyes, then review your reference books for such a chemical compound that may correspond as this?

WATSON: Right away my good man (Watson quickly moves to the desk to work on a simple code)

HOLMES: Mrs. Hudson, tell me exactly what the woman said and did upon her arrival here. Then, please bring a basin of hot water immediately as well.

MRS. HUDSON: Yes... Mr. Holmes... ah... ah

HOLMES: Please, Mrs. Hudson I need more than the stuttering words at the moment.

MRS. HUDSON: Well... yes she entered and asked to see you.

HOLMES: Yes... yes carry on.

MRS. HUDSON: I helped her in...

HOLMES: What do you mean you helped her in?

MRS. HUDSON: I offered her my hand up the last step... she seemed a bit unstable.

HOLMES: You offered...

MRS. HUDSON: Yes, my hand and she took hold of mine with her glove.

HOLMES: I see...

MRS. HUDSON: Then I felt a cool breeze from the outside air, closed the door, I allowed her to collect herself and came to call you... ah, that you had a visitor.

HOLMES: That was it? (Surprised)

MRS. HUDSON: That was it Mr. Holmes. She then made her way up the stairs after some time. Oh aside from that she asked if it was time for tea, which I already had waiting.

HOLMES: Yes... Watson, how are we working along?

WATSON: All those years, at the University of London: the British Army and now this for heaven sake... coming along Holmes.

HOLMES: This poison Watson... airborne I deduce.

WATSON: Yes... (Preoccupied with completing the code) I believe so.

HOLMES: And the antidote... as you observed, this woman had plush sleeves and she removed her gloves, evidentially the form of transmission.

WATSON: Got it Holmes (Watson completes a simple code, then brings it Holmes to review)

HOLMES: Upon my word, Watson, you are coming along wonderfully. You have really done very well indeed. (There is a pause as Holmes ponders) The gloves, the white material... I suspect shows traces.

WATSON: And now upon reflection, the careful placement of those gloves; incidentally she too must have been poisoned then self-administered the antidote.

HOLMES: Watson you may have missed some things of importance, but you have hit upon the method... on the contrary, you do have a quick eye in the visual. We must concentrate upon the details however and find the antidote... I think now would be the time to sit. (Moves to sit squarely in the chair, starting to feel the effects of the poison)

WATSON: Holmes, how are you feeling... anything?

HOLMES: Ah, there's the question, unless I'm very much mistaken, considerably to time, I have approximately seven minutes to live my old friend. That answer would be I am starting to feel the effects just as she wrote... in the legs.

(Mrs. Hudson returns with a bowl of hot water while Watson nervously pushes, then opens and closes reference books on the library shelf)

MRS. HUDSON: I am here Mr. Holmes.

HOLMES: Good Mrs. Hudson, kindly if you don't mind, use a cloth to cool my forehead. (She proceeds to dab his forehead with the warm water)

MRS. HUDSON: He is starting to feel feverish Doctor, Mr. Holmes... this is terrible... just terrible.

HOLMES: Watson... any time now would be good in your referenced search.

WATSON: Yes... Holmes during my army commission, we, by accident uncovered a spore-like substance that turned out to be highly toxic. If my memory serves me our research concluded it remained lethal to those not exposed for just twenty-four hours. (Continues to turn pages if his book)

HOLMES: (With a tone of bitterness) For this, the organizer of half that was evil, a man who creatively aligned with an underworld of criminals, undetected for years... the great Professor Moriarty. And now... who would know his blood relative comes calling.

WATSON: I am looking to retrieve my supplemental notes on the research... here, ah... yes. All right, here it is...

HOLMES: (Grows slightly euphoric) Read on Watson...

WATSON: Ah yes... (Nervously clears his throat) Holmes, we have no choice but to take a chance that the poison is Tricine.

MRS. HUDSON: Tricine... but how can we be sure doctor, in just a matter of minutes or even find an antidote?

WATSON: We cannot...

HOLMES: Correct.

WATSON: According to my notes it's derived from a rare mushroom related spore, resistant, but not impervious, to digestion of any enzyme. By ingestion, the pathology of Tricine is largely restricted to the loss of nervous system functions; progressive muscle movement leading to death if an antidote is not immediately administered.

MRS. HUDSON: We have no choice but to carry on! (It is now obvious that Holmes has lost the use of his legs)

WATSON: I thought at first, it could be perfectly natural in our line of work to be some kind of hoax?

HOLMES: Oh, come now, old fellow, argue the thing out logically. If the letter was genuine, and it is... Handed to Mrs. Hudson herself. Why should she carry it so covertly? She certainly had to time her visit and then hand off the note after the interview. Doesn't it all strike you as rather strange?

MRS. HUDSON: Yes, I suggest Doctor that we spend the immediate time researching an antidote. I will tend to Mr. Holmes.

WATSON: Patience Mrs. Hudson... patience, as I was saying, from the looks of it Holmes is very uncomfortable, now losing his means of reasoning. These chambers have always been full of chemicals references and criminal relics – but his case is our greatest trial of all... I am thinking.

HOLMES: Watson... because the symptoms... (Holmes starting to have difficulty with speech) are caused by failure to... to make protein, they emerge only after an extremely short delay of exposure. Am I correct Watson?

WATSON: Yes, that is what my notes confirm. The only known antidote - never widely tested on humans was developed by the military; made from the pulp of eight bean varieties when processed to a paste.

HOLMES: Extraordinary Watson... and where might we...

MRS. HUDSON: I see he is now finding it difficult to speak Doctor.

WATSON: Go on Holmes... go on!

HOLMES: Might we find the pulp of eight beans... my good man?

WATSON: I am sorry my old friend (With deep emotion), I haven't a clue.

HOLMES: Precisely... the clu... clue (Holmes now seems to be almost completely paralyzed)

WATSON: Now the horror of losing his life to a woman seeking revenge of her father's death. If we ever make it out of this one, I suspect we have another Moriarty to hunt down.

MRS. HUDSON: Doctor... (Breaking down in sorrow) I do not understand... my God! We sit here helpless... while he labors to tell us something.

HOLMES: The clue Watson... concentrate... yourself...

WATSON: Go on Holmes... you can do this (As he moves closer to understand Holmes)

HOLMES: Upon... the... de... details...

WATSON: Mrs. Hudson... Could you please hold this blinking code upwards so Holmes can see it? (Watson gives her the paper containing the code he drafted earlier)

MRS. HUDSON: Yes Doctor...

WATSON: Concentrate yourself upon details... (Thinking) yes. Mrs. Hudson, let us concentrate on the details. Now... from the beginning, she sat down and introduced herself.

MRS. HUDSON: Correct, then I join you with a tea service...

WATSON: Wait, he's now using the code with his eyes... (Watson proceeds to spell the letters from Holmes' blinking eye code) W... H... A... What... what... yes... is card... m... made of? What is the card made of?

Holmes... it looks like some sort of fibrous material. (Responding to Holmes)

T... next word... W... A... warms... the N... nerves: Tea warms the nerves. Yes... Ah yes... precisely old fellow!

MRS. HUDSON: The tea... What in God's name are you talking?

WATSON: Yes, it can be absorbed through the skin or ingested in the form of a brewed tea. (Remembering the research) Mrs. Hudson... quickly... submerge the card she wrote into the cup of hot water... quickly now.

MRS. HUDSON: Yes doctor... (Pours the hot water into a cup and places the card into it) My word... it is turning green!

WATSON: Green... my good lady (Smiling) green! The antidote is effective immediately. Now... please add a few drops to his lips and pat his forehead with it. (She does as he directs) A little more... that is it...

MRS. HUDSON: Amazing... I think he is starting to move his lips... ok Mr. Holmes sip on this... now take your time. (Holmes starts to move slightly) Oh... welcome back Mr. Holmes.

WATSON: Indeed... my old friend... indeed. (Holmes slowly regains mobility)

HOLMES: Thank you Watson, I congratulate you on its discovery. It is of great intrinsic value but of even greater importance as a historical account of the crime.

MRS. HUDSON: But how, Mr. Holmes... how were we all infected with this poison?

HOLMES: Elementary my dear Mrs. Hudson... you helped that along the way.

WATSON: I think what Holmes is saying is that the woman's glove carried the spores. She initially infected you upon her arrival, then sprayed you with the antidote... the cool breeze you spoke of.

HOLMES: Yes correct Watson... then, as for the poison; you proceeded to handle the tea service, which in turn we all handled and that infected us. Watson was also unknowingly administered the antidote upon introduction.

MRS. HUDSON: Fascination... to say the least.

HOLMES: Her hand written not card was made of that very substance... a fibrous material of eight-bean paste fashioned into a paper card. (Holmes now has enough energy to stand walk to desk where he removes an old clay pipe from the rack) Furthermore it wasn't until later oddly enough that I realized the photo she spoke of was the one found on the Professor's body after his death.

WATSON: Holmes you mean to tell me there was actually something that slipped your mind old man?

HOLMES: Evidently, ever so slightly... not much to worry about would you say Mrs. Hudson?

MRS. HUDSON: Oh Mr. Holmes... you will be the death of me yet... we were terribly worried.

HOLMES: Mrs. Hudson... I do so appreciate your dedication. I am feeling much better. Now then... to the matter at hand... Tea anyone? (Smiles)

The End

SHERLOCK HOLMES and THE DARKNESS UPON US

Story by John DeGaetano,
Based on the original books by Sir Arthur Conan Doyle
© July 2012 v:1.3

Type: A Mystery Play
Stage Time Length: 10 Minutes

Cast: 4 men, 2 women:
Set: Flexible Bar / Pub Setting
(Soho District, London England)

Cast of Characters:
SHERLOCK HOLMES
DOCTOR WATSON
INSPECTOR LESTRADE
ANGELA DONATI
JULIET MILLS
HENRY ASTOR

For Stage Production use or more Information
Contact Email: degaetanojohn@yahoo.com
Website: johndegaetanoproductions.com
Phone: 707-338-2886

THE SCENE: (Begins on a hot summer night at the Voodoo Sea Hag, a bar in a seedy area of Soho. Holmes and Dr. Watson are summoned to the scene of a recent murder. Already seated is Inspector Lestrade and Juliet, the cigarette girl)

SOUND: (The sound of footsteps as Holmes and Dr. Watson approach the scene)

HOLMES: Inspector Lestrade looking a bit older than the last time we've set eyes on you. Could it be just the shadows of this late hour?

LESTRADE: Good evening Mr. Holmes... Doctor Watson.

WATSON: Good evening Lestrade.

LESTRADE: Yes, ah I mean no... Scotland yard has been keeping me busy now that we've had a rash of robberies in this area.

HOLMES: Still, you know who he is or at least you think you do. Am I correct Inspector?

LESTRADE: We have our men combing this area as we speak, which I find unusual that any other criminal would care to roam the streets presently and get mixed up in the whole affair.

WATSON: I suspect not so in this case...

LESTRADE: No... not so, this case is completely unrelated.

HOLMES: Inspector I would surmise that you didn't call us to the center of Soho to this fine establishment... (Sarcastic) the Voodoo Sea Hag Pub for a robbery suspect, now did you?

LESTRADE: Ah... well no Mr. Holmes.

WATSON: I knew a hag when I was younger... needless to say we parted ways.

HOLMES: How so my good man?

WATSON: Just not my kind of woman Holmes, a bit crabby and such...

HOLMES: All right then, so why did you call us Inspector, please be so kind as to convince me to stay.

LESTRADE: Murder...

WATSON: Murder?

LESTRADE: That is correct Doctor... murder... here or actually just on the other side of that door to be exact.

HOLMES: I see.

LESTRADE: Mauled...

WATSON: I beg your pardon?

LESTRADE: I said mauled gentlemen, as in an animal. A young fellow was mauled to death by what we think was a tiger.

WATSON: Good heavens... how... a what?

LESTRADE: Your heard that correct Doctor... a tiger. Gentlemen, this is Juliet Mills... she works as the cigarette girl here.

JULIET: Mr. Sherlock Holmes and Doctor Watson... a pleasure to meet you.

LESTRADE: Miss Mills heard the commotion out there and responded to the victim after the attack.

HOLMES: Ah Miss Mills... did you know the victim?

JULIET: No sir…

LESTRADE: His name is Antonio Donati… recently escaped prison. His sister lives not far from here… we have summoned her. She will be here directly.

HOLMES: Miss Mills did the victim do or say anything to you?

JULIET: He did Mr. Holmes… as a matter of fact he did. There was no light in the alley until I opened the door. How could anyone see in such darkness?

HOLMES: And what was it that he said young lady?

JULIET: He said… "Ciechi nell'oscurità di colore."

WATSON: Yes… I see… Italian… Ciechi nell'oscurità di colore.

HOLMES: Correct my good man… "Blind in darkness of color" is the translation.

WATSON: Curious… he spoke his last words in Italian… perhaps the sister can shed some light on him.

HOLMES: Yes, Watson very curious indeed… in fact, any attacker would have to see their victim unless they could see in the dark.

LESTRADE: Something that resembles a tiger… Mr. Holmes?

HOLMES: Actually no cat can see in the dark… they can however see in very low light levels because they have a reflective layer at the back of the eyeball.

WATSON: Correct my good man, the light enters the eye, reflects off the back, then off the front and returns to the back - effectively giving twice as much light to the retina. It also explains Inspector why cat eyes shine in the dark.

LESTRADE: Pure fascination gentlemen...

HOLMES: However my good man, I do not see this to have any bearing on the case except for the attacker and his or her cohort, staking out the area in anticipation of the victim's arrival. (A woman appears at the bar entrance)

LESTRADE: Whoever it was knew the victim would make an appearance here...

HOLMES: That is correct Lestrade. (Miss Donati enters)

LESTRADE: Ah yes... you must be the victim's sister... Miss ah...

ANGELA: Donati... Angela Donati and yes... I am... Antonio was my brother.

WATSON: We are so sorry for your loss Miss Donati.

ANGELA: I knew it... gentlemen... I knew this day would come, fighting and reaching out for a cause... even in prison.

HOLMES: Yes we were told, that he recently escaped, ah... Miss Donati can you be so kind as to tell us why someone would want to harm your brother?

ANGELA: Oh I know exactly why... I'll tell you what I told your sergeant outside. My brother had information... That is why he was constantly threatened in prison and ultimately is why he escaped.

WATSON: Information dear lady... what sort of information?

ANGELA: Several years ago Mr. Holmes there was a man by the name of Gianni Mosca from a small village in central Italy. Tuscany had become a stronghold for radical activity. I know little of the activities of an anarchist group there or Mosca's association. I do know however he served a short sentence in prison as the result of being involved in a political disturbance.

WATSON: Yes, I've read about unrest even to this day over working conditions.

ANGELA: Yes, upon his release Mosca along with others set about introducing ideas to a growing number during an increasingly unstable political and social situation in Italy... My brother was there during the uprising.

HOLMES: I see Miss Donati... was he accused of a crime?

ANGELA: No, no my bother was just a worker in the fields with a wife and small son. As he told it to me the group feared an attack that could leave hundreds dead, so they set out to take action.

WATSON: He must have feared for his family as well?

ANGELA: Yes Doctor.

HOLMES: Continue please... Miss Donati...

ANGELA: Yes... Then at that time, a German Businessman of questionable practices wishing to avenge his own conflicts against the government financed the group. Soon they began to plan an assassination that would hit the highest echelons of the Italian social order...

HOLMES: And that intention was?

ANGELA: The intention was of assassinating... King Umberto I of Italy.

WATSON: My word Miss Donati... the King of Italy?

ANGELA: Yes doctor... there was a quiet hush about this action however this was where the group took a wrong turn in their beliefs. It was a dark time...

WATSON: Inevitably so young lady…

LESTRADE: Your brother still not involved?

ANGELA: That is correct Inspector.

HOLMES: So, your brother merely knew the organizers, and I suspect the sequence of events leading to this point.

ANGELA: Exactly Mr. Holmes. Two months later the plan was foiled and Gianni Mosca was arrested as a key organizer.

WATSON: I see.

ANGELA: The German financier, an executive of industrial growth by the name of Hans Ackerman fled and has never been found. As told by my brother, although suicide was given as the official explanation for Mosca's death in jail before his trial, as not to be implicated in the plan, the order was given by Ackerman himself for Mosca to be killed.

HOLMES: I think what you're trying to say here Miss Donati is that your brother was given information as a safeguard in the event of Mosca's death.

ANGELA: Correct Mr. Holmes… My brother was a friend of Gianni Mosca, separate from the group and consequently given information as where to find Ackerman after his flee from Germany… As I said my brother knew too much.

JULIET: The poor man… I am so sorry for your loss Miss. He had to leave his family?

ANGELA: Yes, he left his family to find his friend's killer, then accused of a crime he didn't commit.

WATSON: That sent him to prison until now.

ANGELA: Correct Doctor... my brother always complained how he was threatened and feared for his life. I believe he escaped prison to find Mosca's killer before someone killed him.

HOLMES: Precisely... Unfortunately he didn't quite accomplish what he came to England for and set out to do.

LESTRADE: Miss Donati... I know this is a difficult time for you, however can I ask you about a few items?

ANGELA: Go right ahead Inspector...

LESTRADE: We found these items on your brother... ah, in his pocket. Do they mean anything to you, (Presents the items) anything at all?

HOLMES: Do you mind Inspector... may I examine these items as well? (They all examine at what looks like a photo and a postal stamp)

LESTRADE: Please go right ahead...

HOLMES: Inspector, by the way, the owner of this establishment... I presume he will be arriving soon?

LESTRADE: That is correct Mr. Holmes, my men have been asked to retrieve him. He should arrive shortly.

WATSON: Let's see... a photo of the victim's sister... that would be you... Miss Donati. (He shows the photo to Angela)

ANGELA: Why yes... yes that is correct.

WATSON: And a postal stamp of the Italian King Umberto I. Ah, yes... but this is a bit unusual?

JULIET: What are you talking about Doctor?

WATSON: Well… this photo, it seems thicker than the usual paper used that of a photographer… wouldn't you say Miss Mills? Anyone else?

JULIET: Why yes Doctor Watson… how very odd. (Hands item to Lestrade)

WATSON: Hello… what is this? (The doctor proceeds to pry a thin film off the back of the photo to reveal what looks like a newspaper clipping)

LESTRADE: It looks like something from a newspaper that was attached to the back of the photo. (They all observe)

HOLMES: Your are absolutely correct Miss Mills… Watson can you make out what it says?

WATSON: The heading reads "Evening Star Reports Businessman Missing" It goes on to say, "British born financier Hans Ackerman wanted for questioning still remains missing."

LESTRADE: Very interesting Doctor Watson, the very subject of our discussion…

WATSON: Yes… there is more. It reads "The man who spent most of his childhood in England set out for Germany to build an empire financing various businesses such as a Salt Cartel, an Italian Canvas Manufacturer, and a Siegfried Bros. Entertainment business remains a mystery as to his whereabouts. No other information is available at this time."

ANGELA: He must have been carrying these items in his possession for years Mr. Holmes.

HOLMES: Yes, Miss Donati… I presume these were his only clues to aid his search.

WATSON: Along with his last words… spoken in Italian.

HOLMES: Correct… (Heavy in thought) However, we do have information, we just have to understand what it means.

ANGELA: Such a senseless murder of a man who had absolutely nothing to do with the uprising in Italy or Mr. Mosca's killer.

WATSON: And we have very little to go on Holmes.

LESTRADE: I agree… I best advise my men to look further look for clues. (He exits side door)

HOLMES: Yes, my dear lady… your brother's death was senseless indeed. (Pauses in thought) Some crimes go without explanation unfortunately… I suspect your brother knew he was getting closer to finding what he was looking for… (Interrupted by the entrance of Henry Astor who picks up the conversation)

MR. ASTOR: However I do hope you find the criminal and we put closure to this whole affair. I do have a business to run.

WATSON: I presume you are?

MR. ASTOR: Yes, I am Henry Astor owner of the Voodoo Sea Hag. I am under the impression that you are the famous Sherlock Holmes and Doctor Watson?

WATSON: Famous to a few perhaps however I put no mind to it. Thank you Mr. Astor for coming.

MR. ASTOR: No mention gentlemen, (Turns to Angela) I am very sorry for your loss madam. I'm sure he was a fine gentleman.

ANGELA: I… I don't know what to say. (Astor attempts to console her)

HOLMES: Mr. Astor... Thank you for allowing us to utilize your business to investigate the crime. You're a busy man, so as a follow up in questioning everyone, I'll get right to the point.

MR. ASTOR: Ah yes, please do, Mr. Holmes.

HOLMES: Is there any way you could have suspected or anticipated for that matter an attack of this type immediately outside your establishment?

MR. ASTOR: Mr. Holmes and Doctor, it is not everyday that a man is attacked by what the police say was a wild animal...

WATSON: Unusual circumstances indeed Mr. Astor.

MR. ASTOR: We have seen many unusual characters in the Hag but nothing more than a fair amount of them in a smoked filled room, a fight or two and a nap in the corner to sleep off the alcohol.

HOLMES: Yes... I see you have quite a selection of liqueurs... enough for one to take several naps. (They chuckle)

MR. ASTOR: That is correct Mr. Holmes I pride myself into having on hand the largest selection in area.

HOLMES: Why I haven't seen such an array of brands since.... Morocco... would you say Watson?

WATSON: I... ah... why yes my good man Morocco... ah, a fond vacation memory you know.

MR. ASTOR: Gentlemen, I am under the impression that my employee Juliet has made you comfortable? Please... let me know if there is any way we can help.

HOLMES: As a matter of fact there is Mr. Astor.

MR. ASTOR: Please... what can I do?

HOLMES: We should be celebrating…

WATSON: We should be?

JULIET: What?

HOLMES: Ah… yes. You see the police are rounding up the killer as we speak.

WATSON: They are? Oh (As an undertone) Why yes…exactly!

MR. ASTOR: Yes… is that so.

HOLMES: That is correct… I see no reason for us to linger here Watson except… in thinking of that Moroccan vacation I certainly could use a small taste of liqueur just to get us on our way home.

MR. ASTOR: Why certainly… what would you like Mr. Holmes?

HOLMES: Do you by chance have Absinthe?

WATSON: Holmes that is likely to send you further than home my good man!

HOLMES: No need to worry Watson.

MR. ASTOR: Very good, yes I do and how about you Dr. Watson?

WATSON: Oh… ah, how about a bit of Red Berry Liqueur?

MR. ASTOR: Oh, a fine choice Doctor. (Astor moves to the bar to pour their requests)

HOLMES: Miss Donati, may we drop you off at your home on our way?

ANGELA: Yes... thank you Mr. Holmes. Would you please...
(Interrupted)

HOLMES: Pay no mind and no worries Miss Donati, I understand
your need to take care of your brother's personal belongings.
Inspector Lestrade can help you with that tomorrow at Scotland
Yard in the light of day.

MR. ASTOR: There you are gentlemen... (Smiles and places the
glasses filled with liqueur on the table) Ah, anything for you, young
lady? (She motions no)

HOLMES: Why thank you... Mr. Astor ever so much. Oh ah... Mr.
Astor... Excuse me but you poured two of the red berry. Remember
mine was Absinthe?

MR. ASTOR: I did? Oh yes, yes I did... I am so sorry. All this
excitement has made me forgetful. Ha, imagine that.

HOLMES: Understandable sir... under the circumstances...

WATSON: Yes indeed.

HOLMES: And thank you Mr. Astor by the way for your fine help in
solving this crime.

MR. ASTOR: What... what are you talking about?

HOLMES: You see the killer or killers I should say were right under
our noses. I suspect you thought a name change would erase the
past, now did you not?

MR. ASTOR: I don't understand where this is going Mr. Holmes but I
warn you... you are making a terrible mistake.

HOLMES: Give yourself up Mr. Henry Astor... let us all go home.
(Astor now pulls a pistol out of his pocket vest and proceeds to back
up towards the door, everyone is now frightened) You see Absinthe a

green liqueur and Red Berry liqueur of course is red... you were correct in what you originally poured. Ciechi nell'oscurità di colore means blind in darkness of color... the translation that...you sir, are... colorblind.

MR. ASTOR: Back... stand back everyone. (Waves his gun)

LESTRADE: I wouldn't do that Mr. Astor if I were you or should I say... Mr. Hans Ackerman. (Lestrade appears in the doorway behind Astor and removes the gun from his hand)

HOLMES: You see, an individual such as yourself with this form of blindness is not actually blind to both red and green at the same time, but rather either the red, or green colors. The outcome is however the same, an inability to tell the difference.

LESTRADE: You... Mr. Ackerman are accused of the murder of Mr. Gianni Mosca and conspiracy.

HOLMES: Yes, and as for Antonio Donati, I suspect it's only a matter of time we pick up his murderer... That would be one of the Siegfried brothers as mentioned in the article we found on the victim.

WATSON: Yes the famous Siegfried Brothers German Circus, I might add... and their assortment of wild animals. I suspect they owed you a favor?

MR. ASTOR: But how... how could you...

HOLMES: The article found on the victim stated your interests in a canvas manufacturer... one that could supply the materials for canvas tents, consequently for your other investment... in the entertainment field. So the association to the circus gave it away.

LESTRADE: Excellent work Mr. Holmes...

ANGELA: And... thank you Mr. Holmes... for lifting the darkness upon us.

HOLMES: You are very welcome...

WATSON: I was just starting to like this place... and the name Voodoo Sea Hag. More than I can say for the last hag I had the distasteful pleasure of knowing. (Chuckles)

JULIET: Mr. Holmes, Doctor Watson, we can't thank you enough...

HOLMES: Thanks to you Miss Donati, and also to you Miss Mills... our work is done here... (Turns to Lestrade)

You're in good hands with Inspector Lestrade... Mr. Hans Ackerman.

LESTRADE: All right, it's off you go sir... (Escorts him out)

The End

More Plays Available by John DeGaetano

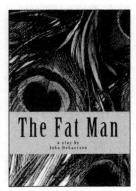

THE FAT MAN - Set as a 1950's radiobroadcast rehearsal in a basement studio on the outskirts of New York City. As a result, the performers hilariously uncover what it's like to all be in the same room with each other or in this case a basement and experience the true test of patience as they nervously prepare for a live performance. (Comedy, 2 Acts)

AVERAGE JOE - A common classic story await as you're taken back to now... to present day issues and a grass roots movement in the fast paced world of media overload and economic turmoil, something we can all identify with. (Comedy, 2 Acts)

ONCE UPON... A CRIME - Everything you've ever known to expect from a somewhat screwball comedy slash courtroom drama. What we mean is everything hits the fan as Attorney Sam Wilson attempts to solve a case that goes beyond what he can remember. (Comedy, 2 Acts)

SHERLOCK HOLMES AND THE PRINCESS JEWEL - The world's greatest detective reaches out in an all-new adventure to solve a 200-year old secret in one of the most important cases of his remarkable career that is too tempting to ignore. (Mystery, 2 Acts)

A SITUATION IN SAFE HAVEN - A crooked bank executive, a mobster, a nun and a guy who commercializes the witness protection program all converge on a tiny town in Northern California. The result is havoc as Jenny and Stanley remove themselves from their previous lives and attempt to start a family. (Comedy, 2 Acts)

For more information on these and other items please visit our website: johndegaetanoproductions.com

CPSIA information can be obtained
at www.ICGtesting.com
Printed in the USA
LVOW05s2135050117
519936LV00012B/690/P